WHITNEY'S

HIGH SIERRA

BY PROF. JOSIAH D. WHITNEY

Reprinted from Josiah D. Whitney's

"The Yosemite Guide Book"

Published In 1870

Cover and other photographs by
Thomas H. Griffin

SENTINEL PUBLICATIONS
Box 367
Ramona, California 92065

INDEX OF PHOTOGRAPHS

6. Photograph of Josiah D. Whitney in his later years.
12. Packers cooling off at Rainbow Falls.
20. Fishing a beautiful pool in Cascade Valley.
23. Log bridge on trail to East Lake, near Bridgeport.
27. The placid Merced meanders thru Yosemite Valley.
31. Trail thru talus on Duck Pass.
39. Inviting, wild backcountry deep in the Sierra.
43. Weather threatens over backcountry lake.
47. Forest area on the trail to Virginia lake.
51. Starting the ascent out of Cascade Valley.
55. Headin' for Tully's Hole and base camp.
68. On top of Tioga Pass, going west.
    Whitney's geological group.

Cover Photo: Purple Lake
August 1953

Foreword

Possibly no mountain in the Western Hemisphere is more widely-known than California's Mt. Whitney, a name which evokes visions of glittering and resplendent peaks. The mountain received the appellation in 1864 in honor of a man of stature, not a shade less than the peak itself, Josiah Dwight Whitney.

Much criticized by devotees of the John Muir memorabilia for his theories about glacial erosion in the Yosemite, which did not parallel those of Muir, Professor Whitney still was the most distinguished American geologist of his period. In recommending Professor Whitney's qualifications to the California State Legislature, which was considering Whitney's appointment as State Geologist, the great Louis Agassiz said that he "has no equal in the United States." (Brewster's Life and Letters of Josiah Dwight Whitney (1909)). Brewster held that Whitney "had Dana's learning and Le Conte's skill, and in field experience, he surpassed both."

With Muir disciples the chief point of dis-praise seems to have become that Professor Whitney failed to be impressed with the apparent glacial action in the Sierra Nevada. The magnificence of John Muir certainly did not require the disparagement of Whitney by Muir partisans. But a character study is perhaps thought to be enhanced and the quintessence of the vignette strengthened, if an element of polemics is introduced, justified or not. And for emotional appeal a Burke must be dredged up for every Paine and for every Disraeli a Gladstone.

Lampoonery can never cloak Professor Whitney's sound professional work as State Geologist. He added to the geological map the State of California, and much of Washington, Nevada and Oregon.

The professor performed a phenomenal feat against formidable odds, the greatest challenge being the extracting of operating money from a disinterested legislature. He was once forced to pay expenses and assistants' salaries out of his own funds. Whitney began the California Survey in 1860—61 with the paltry allotment of $10,000, and yet was able through his assistants' respect for his brilliance and professionalism to assemble a company of scientists and workers of the highest calibre. Though underpaid, the scientists and their leader lived a laborious but happy existence. There was a strong bond between Whitney and his self-denying assistants, who gave him affection, esteem (which amounted almost to awe) and loyalty.

The professor's principal assistants were: William M. Gabb, paleontologist; William Ashburner, assistant in geology; C. F. Hoffmann, assistant and topographer; Chester Averill, engineering assistant; William H. Brewer, chemist and botanist; and Clarence King, geological assistant. The names are familiar to Sierra wilderness travelers, for mountains have been named for most of these men.

Josiah Whitney's contribution to California and to science in general was monumental. The scientific world of the period was most appreciative of and complimentary about his work, awarding him multitudinous honors both here and in Europe. In subsequent years, the single issue of the glacial theory of Yosemite Valley has relegated Whitney to near obscurity behind Muir, who made his own kind of contribution to the state and to science. This is unfortunate.

Thomas H. Griffin

San Diego, California 1971

About This Book

"Nothing so refines the ideas, purifies the heart, and exalts the imagination . . . ," said Professor Josiah D. Whitney of the mountains of the High Sierra. Nothing of the sculptured imagery of the poet is extant here, for Whitney was a scientist, at once and finally.

The professor fitted the characteristic mold of the brilliant and trenchantly-analytical scientist, but his continual acknowledgement of the aesthetics of the glorious scenes around him indicate that he loved them, and this is clearly evident in his "High Sierra" narrative. This love will be appreciated by those who have deep affection for the Sierra and by mountain-minded people everywhere. One soon discovers that the account of the range's early exploration by Whitney and party is irresistibly fascinating, and his easy grace of statement a pleasure to read.

The reader travels with the Whitney geological survey party through the heart of the Sierra in that wonderful time when no trails existed except for an infrequent arterial path from east to west. He may vicariously experience the exhilaration prompted by each new and grand vista which revealed itself to the party. Those familiar with the Sierra Nevada may find it impossible to realize that this book was written in 1869, so vivid and alive is its flavor for the reader today.

Devotees of the High Sierra will soon be apprised that much of the nomenclature of the range was established in that exploration known as the California Geological Survey. With many-faceted interests — historical, scientific, adventurous and personal — Whitney's "High Sierra" is a classic in Americana and mountaineering. It is a grand adventure!

In his prefatory note to the "Yosemite Guide-Book", from which Whitney's "High Sierra" is reprinted, Professor Whitney made reference to two editions of the book, one illustrated with photographs and the other with exquisite woodcuts. The woodcuts are reproduced in this book. The publishers were delighted that the original woodcuts were enhanced by enlargement in the lithographic process, and that the original type faces were rendered more readable with enlargement.

Note: The reader should disregard mileage computations, altitudes recorded and related data in this book. Subsequent findings, with more sophisticated scientific apparatus, have superseded the California Geological Survey's original records.

T.H.G.

Josiah D. Whitney

THE HIGH SIERRA

We call the reader's attention to the higher region of the Sierra Nevada — the Alps of California, as the upper portion of this great chain of mountains is sometimes called; this region we designate, for convenience, as the "High Sierra." It is, however, especially the elevated valleys and mountains which lie above and near the Yosemite that we wish to describe, and to endeavor to bring to the reader's notice, as this is not only a region central and easy of access, but one extremely picturesque, and offering to the lover of high mountain scenery every possible inducement for a visit. By adding a few more days to the time required for a trip to the Yosemite, the tourist may make himself acquainted with a type of scenery quite different from that of countries usually visited by pleasure travellers, and may enjoy the sight of as lofty snow-covered peaks, and as grand panoramic views of mountain and valley, as he can find in Switzerland itself. This region of the High Sierra in California is hardly yet opened to visitors, so far as the providing for them of public accommodations is concerned, for there is not a hotel, nor a permanently inhabited house, anywhere near the crest of the Sierra, between the Silver Mountain road on the north and Walker's Pass on the south; but such is the mildness of the summer, and so steady is the clearness of the atmosphere in the Californian high mountains, that, with a very limited amount of preparation, one may make the tour outside of the Yosemite almost without any discomforts, and certainly without any danger. In the Sierra Nevada, the entire absence of severe storms during the summer, and the almost uninterrupted serenity of the sky, particularly invite to pleasure travel. The worrying delays and the serious risks of Alpine travel, caused by long-continued rains and storms of wind and hail, with their attendant

7

avalanches of snow and rocks, are unknown in the Californian high mountains, and we have camped by the week together, in the constant enjoyment of the finest weather, at elevations which would seem too great for anything but hardship and discomfort.

A comparison of the Swiss and Californian Alpine scenery is not easy, and yet it seems natural to wish to give some idea of the most striking features of the Sierra by referring for comparison, or contrast, to the mountain scenery of Switzerland, which has become the very focus of pleasure travel for the civilized world.*

The much smaller quantity of snow and ice in the Sierra, as compared with regions of equal elevation in Switzerland, is the most striking feature of difference between the mountains of the two countries. In the Sierra we see almost exactly what would be presented to view in the Alps, if the larger portion of the ice and snow-fields were melted away. The marks of the old glaciers are there; but the glaciers themselves are gone. The polished surfaces of the rocks, the moraines or long trains of detritus, and the striæ engraved on the walls of the cañons, — these speak eloquently of such an icy covering once existing here as now clothes the summits of the Alps.

Another feature of the Sierra, as compared with the Alps, is the absence of the "Alpen," or those grassy slopes which occur above the line of forest vegetation, between that and the eternal snow, and which have given their names to the mountains themselves. In the place of these, we have in the California mountains the forests extending quite up to the snow-line in many places, and everywhere much higher than in the Alps. The forests of the Sierra, and especially at elevations of 5,000 to 7,000 feet, are magnificent, both in the size and beauty of the trees, and far beyond any in the Alps; they constitute one of the most attractive features of the scenery, and yet they are somewhat monotonous in their uniformity of type, and they give a sombre tone to the landscape, as seen from a distance in their dark shades of green. The grassy valleys, along the streams, are extremely beautiful, but occupy only a small area; and, especially, they do not produce a marked effect in the distant views, since they are mostly concealed behind the ranges, to one looking over the country from a high point.

* There are probably ten times as many persons in California who have travelled for pleasure in Switzerland, as among these most interesting portions of the Sierra.

The predominating features, then, of the High Sierra are sublimity and grandeur, rather than beauty and variety. The scenery will perhaps produce as much impression, at first, as that of the Alps, but will not invite so frequent visits, nor so long a delay among its hidden recesses. Its type is different from that of the Swiss mountains, and should be studied by those who wish to see Nature in all her variety of mountain gloom and mountain glory. The many in this country who do not have the opportunity of seeing the Alps should not miss the Sierra, if it be in their power to visit it.

For a journey around the Yosemite, or in any portion of the High Sierra, mules or horses may be hired at Bear Valley, Mariposa, or Coulterville; and the services of some one who will act as guide can be obtained, usually, at either of these places. But there are, as yet, no regular guides for the high mountains, and travel must increase considerably before any such will be found. A good pedestrian will often prefer to walk, and will pack his baggage on a horse or mule. For convenience and enjoyment, the party should consist of several persons. A good supply of blankets and of provisions, with a few simple cooking utensils, an axe, a light tent, substantial woollen clothes, and, above all, or rather under all, a pair of boots "made on honor," with the soles filled with nails, — these are the principal requisites. The guide will initiate the unpractised traveller into the mysterious art of "packing" a mule or horse, an accomplishment which can only be acquired by actual practice, but one on the skilful performance of which much of the traveller's comfort depends. Those who are familiar with woods-life in California, or elsewhere, can easily find their way about with the help of the maps contained in this volume.

It will be the principal object of this chapter to describe the region of the High Sierra adjacent to the Yosemite, and this will first be done; after which, we will add a brief description of some other less known portions of the Sierra, in the hope that travellers may be induced to visit them, and, perhaps, to give to the world some of their experience, for the benefit of future tourists. And, for convenience, we will first describe the trip which is most likely to be made by those visiting the Yosemite; namely, an excursion around the Valley, on the outside, one which will reveal much that is of great interest, occupying but few days, and which can be made mostly on beaten trails, without the slightest difficulty or danger. We cannot but believe that the time will soon come when hundreds, if not thousands, will every year visit this region, and that it will become as well known as the valleys and peaks of the Bernese Oberland.

In making the circuit of the Yosemite, as here proposed, the traveller is supposed to start from the Valley itself, leaving it on the north side, and following the Mono trail to Soda Springs, camping there and ascending Mount Dana, then returning by the trail from Mono to Mariposa, passing behind Cloud's Rest and the Half Dome, through the Little Yosemite, across the Illilouette, by the Sentinel Dome, then to Westfall's and back into the Valley, or to Clark's Ranch, as may be desired, the whole trip occupying about a week.

Leaving the Valley, the traveller ascends to the plateau by the Coulterville trail; but, instead of keeping on the trail back to that place, turns sharp to the right just after passing the Boundary corner, taking the trail formerly considerably used by mule-trains between Big Oak Flat and Aurora. This trail was of some importance at the time that the Esmeralda District was in favor with mining speculators; for, although it rises to the elevation of over 10,700 feet above the sea-level, yet, there being an abundance of feed at the various flats and meadows on the route, — which, as they were not claimed or fenced in, were free to all, — it offered a more eligible route for large trains of mules than the passes farther north, where all the grass was taken possession of by settlers, and where, consequently, feed must be purchased. In 1863 all the meadows on the Silver Mountain road (the one next north of the Sonora Pass road) were claimed; there were several public houses on the route, and a public conveyance over it; but, at that time, there was not a house or a settler on the Mono trail anywhere between Deer Flat, twenty-two miles below the Yosemite, and the eastern base of the Sierra, near Mono Lake; nor is there now, so far as we are informed. The traveller, therefore, will not be able to telegraph, in advance of his arrival, for rooms at the sumptuous hotel at the next station; but he will find grassy meadows in which to pasture his animals, scattered along the route at convenient intervals, will have an abundance of ice-cold water, and, drawing on his saddle-bags for his own rations, with unlimited command of free fuel, he will find both novelty and delight in his entire independence of hotel bills, and in knowing that he is not in danger of being crowded out of his " accommodations."

10

The first good camping-ground, after leaving the Valley on the Mono trail, is in the neighborhood of the Virgin's Tears Creek, and from here the highest of the Three Brothers may be easily reached, in an hour or two. There is no trail blazed as yet; but the shortest and best way can easily be found, in the absence of a guide, by the aid of the map. From this commanding point, almost 4,000 feet above the Valley, the view is extremely fine, the Merced River and green meadows which border it seeming to be directly under the observer's feet. Probably there is no better place from which to get a bird's-eye view of the Yosemite Valley itself; and, in respect to the distant view of the Sierra to be had from the summit of the Three Brothers, it can only be said, that, like all the others which can be obtained from commanding positions around the Valley, it seems, while one is enjoying it, to be the finest possible. At the time of our visit to this region in 1866, we climbed a commanding ridge just north of our camp on the Virgin's Tears Creek, from which a noble panoramic view of the Sierra was had. It was just at sunset, and the effect of color which was produced by some peculiar condition of the atmosphere, and which continued for at least a quarter of an hour, was something entirely unique and indescribably beautiful. The whole landscape, even the foreground and middle ground, as well as the distant ranges, became of a bright Venetian-red color, producing an effect which a painter would vainly attempt to imitate by any color or combination of colors. It was unlike the "Alpine glow," so often seen in high mountains; for, instead of being confined to the distant and lofty ranges, it tinged even the nearest objects, and not with shades of rose-color and purple, but with a uniform tint of brilliant, clear red.

After crossing the Virgin's Tears, the next creek is that which forms the Yosemite Falls, and which is about two miles farther on. The trail crosses this creek a little above a small meadow, where one can camp, and from which the brink of the fall and the summit of the cliff overhanging it on the east may be visited. A couple of miles farther on is a high meadow called Deer Park, on which there was some snow even in the latter part of June, 1863; for we are here nearly 8,500 feet above the sea-level. Descending a little, we soon reach Porcupine Flat, a small meadow of carices, 8,173 feet above tide-water, and a good camping-ground for those who wish to visit Mount Hoffmann.

Packers cooling off at Rainbow Falls, near Red's Meadow

Mount Hoffmann is the culminating point of a group of elevations, very conspicuous from various points about the Yosemite, and especially from the Mariposa trail and from Sentinel Dome, looking directly across the Valley and to the north of it. It is about four miles northwest of Porcupine Flat, and can be reached and ascended without the slightest difficulty. The ridge to which it belongs forms the divide between the head-waters of Tenaya and Yosemite Creeks, the latter heading in several small lakes which lie immediately under the bold mural face of the range, which is turned to the northwest. The summit is 10,872 feet above the sea-level, and is a bare granitic mass, with a gently curving slope on the south side, but falling off in a grand precipice to the north.

The view from the summit of Mount Hoffmann is remarkably fine, and those who have not time, or inclination, to visit the higher peaks of the main ridge of the Sierra are strongly advised to ascend this, as the trip from the Yosemite and back need only occupy two or three days; and no one who has not climbed some high point above the Valley can consider himself as having made more than a distant acquaintance with the High Sierra. This is a particularly good point for getting an idea of the almost inaccessible region of volcanic masses lying between the Tuolumne River and the Sonora Pass road, of which a characteristic instance is given in Fig. 9, which represents some of the great tables resting on the granite and 3,000 feet above the adjacent valley, the dark mass of lava in the centre of the picture being fully 700 feet thick. The number of distinct peaks, ridges, and tables, visible in that direction, crowded together, is too great to be counted. The grand mass of Castle Peak is a prominent and most remarkably picturesque object. This mountain was thus named by Mr. G. H. Goddard, about ten years ago, at which time he ascended, by estimate, to within 1,000 feet of the summit, and calculated it to be 13,000 feet in elevation above the sea-level.* Messrs. King and Gardner made several attempts to climb it, but did not succeed in getting to the top, although Mr. Goddard thinks it can easily be reached from the north. By some unaccountable mistake, the name of Castle Peak was afterwards transferred to a rounded and not at all

* Mr. Goddard's measurement was made with an aneroid barometer, and subsequent examinations along his route, by the Geological Survey, indicate that his figures are about 500 feet too great. Castle Peak is probably between 12,000 and 12,500 feet high.

VOLCANIC TABLES ON GRANITE.

castellated mass about seven miles north of Mount Dana; but we have
returned the name to the peak to which it belongs, and given that of General
Warren, the well-known topographer and engineer, to the one on which the
entirely unsuitable name of Castle Peak had become fixed.

From Porcupine Flat and Mount Hoffmann, we look directly south on to
the fine group of mountains lying southeast of the Yosemite and called by
us the Obelisk Group, which will be fully described further on in this chapter. (See Plate IV.) It is a conspicuous feature in the scenery of the
region about the Yosemite.

Lake Tenaya, the head of the branch of the Merced of the same name, is
the next point of interest on the trail, and is about six miles east-northeast
of Porcupine Flat. It is a beautiful sheet of water, a mile long and half
a mile wide. The trail passes around its east side, and good camping-ground
can be found at the upper end in a fine grove of firs and pines. The rocks
in the vicinity all exhibit in the most remarkable degree the concentric
structure peculiar to the granite of this region. At the head of the
Lake is a very conspicuous conical knob of smooth granite, about 800 feet

PLATE IV.

THE OBELISK GROUP — FROM PORCUPINE FLAT.

high, entirely bare of vegetation, and beautifully scored and polished by former glaciers. The traces of the existence of an immense flow of ice down the valley now occupied by Lake Tenaya begin here to be very conspicuous. The ridges on each side of the trail are worn and polished by glacial action nearly to their summits, so that travelling really becomes difficult for the animals on the pass from the valley of the Tenaya into that of the Tuo-

Fig. 10.

CATHEDRAL PEAK, FROM NEAR LAKE TENAYA.

lumne, so highly polished and slippery are the broad areas of granite over which they have to pick their way. A branch of the great Tuolumne glacier flowed over into the Tenaya Valley through this pass, showing that the thickness of the mass of ice was much more than 500 feet, which is the difference of level between the summit of the pass and the Tuolumne River. As the glacial markings are seen on the rocks around Lake Tenaya at an elevation of fully 500 feet above its level, it is certain that the whole thickness of the ice in the Tuolumne Valley must have been at least 1,000 feet. The summit of the pass is 9,070 feet above the sea-level.

The trail descends into the valley of the Tuolumne, winding down under the brow of the Cathedral Peak group, a superb mass of rock, which first becomes conspicuously visible to the traveller just before reaching Lake

16

Tenaya. (See Fig. 10.) This is one of the grandest land-marks in the whole region, and has been most appropriately named. As seen from the west and southwest, it presents the appearance of a lofty mass of rock, cut squarely down on all sides for more than a thousand feet, and having at its southern end a beautiful cluster of slender pinnacles, which rise several hundred feet above the main body. It requires no effort of the imagination to see the

Fig. 9.

CATHEDRAL PEAK, FROM TUOLUMNE VALLEY.

resemblance of the whole to a Gothic cathedral; but the majesty of its form and its vast dimensions are such, that any work of human hands would sink into insignificance beside it. Its summit is at least 2,500 feet above the surrounding plateau, and about 11,000 feet above the sea-level. From the Tuolumne River Valley, on the east, the Cathedral Peak presents a most attractive appearance; but has quite lost the peculiar resemblance which was so conspicuous on the other side. (See Fig. 11 and Plate V.)

17

Unicorn Peak.

Cathedral Peak.

UPPER TUOLUMNE VALLEY — FROM SODA SPRINGS, LOOKING SOUTH.

18

The valley of the Tuolumne, into which the Mono trail now descends (see map), is one of the most picturesque and delightful in the High Sierra. Situated at an elevation of between 8,000 and 9,000 feet above the sea-level, surrounded by noble ranges and fantastically shaped peaks which rise from 3,000 to 4,000 feet higher, and from which the snow never entirely disappears, traversed by a clear rapid river, along which meadows of carices and clumps of pines and firs alternate, the effect of the whole is indeed most superb. The main portion of the valley is about four miles long, and from half to a third of a mile wide. At its upper end it forks, the Mono trail taking the left-hand branch, or that which comes down from Mount Dana, while the right-hand fork, or that which enters from the southeast, is the one heading on the north side of Mount Lyell (see map), about eight miles above the junction of the two branches. Soda Springs, on the north side of the Tuolumne, near the place where the Mono trail descends into the valley, offers an agreeable camping-ground, and many other pleasant spots can be found between this and the head of the pass. The springs furnish a mild chalybeate water, slightly impregnated with carbonic acid gas, and rather pleasant to the taste. They are elevated thirty or forty feet above the river, and are 8,680 feet above the sea. From this point the view in all directions is a magnificent one. The Cathedral Peak Group is one of the most conspicuous features in the landscape, the graceful, slender form of the dominating peak being always attractive, from whichever side it is seen. What resembled the spires of a cathedral, in the distant view from the west, near Lake Tenaya, is now seen to be two bare pyramidal peaks, rising precipitously from the forest-clothed sides of the ridge to the height of about 2,300 feet above the valley. (See Plate V.) Farther east the range is continued in a line of jagged peaks and pinnacles, too steep for the snow to remain upon them, and rising above great slopes of bare granite, over which, through the whole summer, large patches of snow are distributed, in sheltered places and on the north side. One of these peaks has a very peculiar horn-shaped outline, and hence was called Unicorn Peak. This range trends off to the southeast and unites with the grand mass of the Mount Lyell Group, which forms the dominating portion of the Sierra in this region.

The vicinity of Soda Springs, and, indeed, the whole region about the head of the upper Tuolumne, is one of the finest in the State for studying

Fishing a beautiful pool in Cascade Valley where fish are abundant, but small

20

the traces of the ancient glacier system of the Sierra Nevada. The valleys of both the Mount Lyell and the Mount Dana forks exhibit abundant evidence of having been filled, at no very remote period, with an immense body of moving ice, which has everywhere rounded and polished the surface of the rocks, up to at least a thousand feet above the level of the river. This polish extends over a vast area, and is so perfect that the surface

Fig. 12.

GLACIER-POLISHED ROCKS, UPPER TUOLUMNE VALLEY.

is often seen from a distance to glitter with the light reflected from it, as from a mirror. Not only have we these evidences of the former existence of glaciers, but all the phenomena of the moraines — lateral, medial, and terminal — are here displayed on the grandest scale.

To the northeast of Soda Springs, a plateau stretches along the south-western side of the crest of the Sierra, with a gentle inclination towards the river, rising gradually up to a rugged mass of peaks, of which Mount Conness is the highest. The plateau lies at an elevation of between 9,000 and 10,000 feet; it has clumps of *Pinus contorta* scattered over it, and is furrowed by water-courses, which are not very large. The whole surface of this is most beautifully polished and grooved, except where covered with the piles of *débris*, which stretch across it in long parallel lines, and which are the medial moraines of the several side glaciers, which formerly united with the main one, coming down from the gorges and cañons of the great mass of the Sierra above. About a mile below the springs are the remains of a terminal moraine, stretching across the valley; it is not very conspicuous, except from the fact that it bears a scattered growth of pines, contrasting beautifully with the grassy and level area above and below. A mile and a half lower down, a belt of granite, a mile or more wide, extends across the valley; over this the river falls in a series of cascades, having a perpendicular descent of above a hundred feet in all. This granite belt is worn into many knobs, some of which are a hundred feet high and over; between these are great grooves and channels worn by ice, and their whole surface, to the very summit, is scratched and polished, the markings being parallel with the present course of the river.

Below this is another grassy field, and then the river enters a cañon, which is about twenty miles long, and probably inaccessible through its entire length; at least we have never heard of its being explored, and it certainly cannot be entered from its head. Mr. King followed this cañon down as far as he could, to where the river precipitated itself down in a grand fall, over a mass of rock so rounded on the edge, that it was impossible to approach near enough to look over into the chasm below, the walls on each side being too steep to be climbed. Where the cañon opens out again, twenty miles below, so as to be accessible, a remarkable counterpart of the Yosemite Valley is found, called the Hetch-Hetchy Valley, which will be described farther on. Between this and Soda Springs there is a descent in the river of 4,500 feet, and what grand waterfalls and stupendous scenery there may be here it is not easy to say. Although we have not succeeded in getting into this cañon, it does not follow that it cannot be done. Adventurous climbers, desirous of signalizing themselves by new discoveries, should try to penetrate into this unknown gorge, which may perhaps admit of being entered through some of the side cañons coming in from the north, and

22

Backcountry trails in the High Sierra are adequately maintained, and well-marked. Log bridge on the trail to East Lake, near Bridgeport.

which must exhibit stupendous scenery. The region north of this cañon, as far as the Sonora road across the Sierra, is wonderfully wild and difficult of access. Our parties made some attempt to penetrate it, and to reach Castle Peak, but without success, partly owing to the great difficulty of finding feed for the animals.

Just before reaching the head of the great cañon, there is an isolated granite knob in the valley, rising to the height of about 800 feet above the river, and beautifully glacier-polished to its very summit. At this point the great glacier of the Tuolumne must have been at least a mile and a half wide and over 1,000 feet thick. From this knob the view of the valley and the surrounding mountains is one hardly surpassed in interest and grandeur. Plate VI. reproduces a sketch taken from this point looking towards the Cathedral Peak Group, and shows the fine mass of elevations to the southwest. In the lower part of the valley are the smooth and glittering surfaces of granite, indicating the former existence of the glacier; above this, on either hand, the steep slopes of the mountains, clad with a sombre growth of pines (*Pinus contorta*), and beyond, still higher up, the great snow-fields, above which rises the Unicorn Peak, and many other nameless ones, in grand contrast with the dome-shaped masses seen, in the farthest distance, in the direction of Lake Tenaya.

Of all the excursions which can be made from Soda Springs, the one most to be recommended is the ascent of Mount Dana, as being entirely without difficulty or danger, and as offering one of the grandest panoramic views which can be had in the Sierra Nevada; those who wish to try a more difficult feat can climb Mount Lyell or Mount Conness.* Since the visit of the Geological Survey to this region, in 1863, several parties have ascended Mount Dana, riding nearly to the summit on horseback, and there can be no doubt that the ascent will, in time, become well known, and popular among tourists. As it is rather too hard a day's work to go from

* Mount Dana was named after Professor J. D. Dana, the eminent American geologist; Mount Lyell, from Sir Charles Lyell, whose admirable geological works have been well known to students of this branch of science, in this country, for the past thirty years. Mount Conness bears the name of a distinguished citizen of California, now a United States Senator, who deserves, more than any other person, the credit of carrying the bill organizing the Geological Survey of California, through the Legislature, and who is chiefly to be credited for another great scientific work, the Survey of the 40th Parallel.

24

PLATE VI.

CATHEDRAL PEAK GROUP — UPPER TUOLUMNE VALLEY.

Soda Springs to the summit of Mount Dana and back in a day, it will be convenient to move camp to the base of the mountain, near the head of the Mono Pass. The distance from the springs to the summit of the pass is about ten miles in a straight line, and perhaps twelve in following the trail. A convenient place for camping, and from which to ascend Mount Dana, is at a point about three miles from the summit of the pass, on the left bank of the stream and near the junction of a small branch, coming in from the slopes of Mount Dana to unite with the main river, which heads in the pass itself and along the ridges to the southeast of it. This camp is 9,805 feet above the sea, and about a thousand feet below the summit of the pass, which is 10,765 feet in elevation.

An examination of the map will give a better idea than any verbal explanation can do of the character and position of the subordinate members of the crest of the Sierra in this region. A jagged line of granite pinnacles runs from the head of the San Joaquin River northwest, for about twenty miles, beginning at the Minarets and ending at Cathedral Peak. Mount Ritter, Mount Lyell, and Mount Maclure are the only points in this range that we have named; * they are all about 13,000 feet high.

From Mount Lyell starts off a grand spur connecting with the Obelisk Group Range, which runs parallel with the Mount Lyell Range and about ten miles from it. About the same distance from the latter, in the opposite direction from the Obelisk Group, is another serrated line of peaks, of which Mount Conness is the culminating point. Connecting the Mount Lyell and the Mount Conness ranges, and forming the main divide of the Sierra, in this part, is a series of elevations which have rounded summits and rather gently sloping sides, contrasting in the most marked manner with the pinnacles and obelisks of the other ranges. This portion of the Sierra runs north and south, and has as its dominating mass Mount Dana, which appears to be the highest point anywhere in this region, and which was, for a considerable time, supposed by us to be the highest of the whole Sierra, with the exception of Mount Shasta. Mount Dana and Mount Lyell are so nearly of the same height that the difference falls within the limits of possible

* Ritter is the name of the great German geographer, the founder of the science of modern comparative geography. To the pioneer of American geology, William Maclure, one of the dominating peaks of the Sierra Nevada is very properly dedicated.

The placid Merced meanders through woods and fields of pleasantness, in Yosemite.

instrumental error; but on levelling, with a pocket-level, from one to the other, the former seemed to be a little the higher of the two.

Mount Dana is the second peak north of the pass; the one between that mountain and the pass is called Mount Gibbs. Between the two is a gap somewhat lower than the Mono Pass, but descending too steeply on the eastern side to admit of use without considerable excavation. There is also another pass on the north side of Mount Dana, as represented on the map; this is about 600 feet lower than the Mono Pass, and might probably be made available with a small expenditure. From the summit everywhere to the east, the descent is exceedingly rapid; that through "Bloody Cañon," as the east slope of the Mono Pass is called, lets the traveller down 4,000 feet in three miles. The total descent from the summit of Mount Dana to Mono Lake is 6,773 feet, and the horizontal distance only six miles, or over 1,100 feet fall to the mile.

We ascended Mount Dana twice from the south side without difficulty, sliding down on the snow for a considerable portion of the way, on the return, making a descent of about 1,200 feet in a couple of minutes. We have been told, however, that the approach to the summit from the opposite side is much easier, and that it is even possible to ride a horse nearly to the top from the northwest. The height was determined by us to be 13,227 feet, and it need hardly be added that the view from the summit is sublime. Every tourist who wishes to make himself acquainted with the high mountain scenery of California should climb Mount Dana; those who ascend no higher than the Yosemite, and never penetrate into the heart of the mountains, should never undertake to talk of having seen the Sierra Nevada;—as well claim an intimate acquaintance with the Bernese Oberland after having spent a day or two in Berne, or with Mont Blanc after visiting Geneva. The Yosemite is something by itself; it is not the High Sierra, it belongs to an entirely different type of scenery. From Mount Dana, the innumerable peaks and ranges of the Sierra itself, stretching off to the north and south, form, of course, the great feature of the view. To the east, Mono Lake lies spread out, as on a map, at a depth of nearly 7,000 feet below, while beyond it rise, chain above chain, the lofty and, here and there, snow-clad ranges of the Great Basin,—a region which may well be called a wilderness of mountains, barren and desolate in the highest degree, but possessing many of the

28

PLATE VII.

Mount Dana.

Glacier-polished surfaces.

CREST OF THE SIERRA, LOOKING EAST FROM ABOVE SODA SPRINGS.

29

elements of the sublime, especially vast extent and wonderful variety and grouping of mountain forms.

The upper part of Mount Dana is not granite, as are almost all the surrounding peaks. It is made up of slate, very metamorphic near the summit, and showing, farther down, especially on the south side, alternating bands of bright green and deep reddish-brown, and producing a very pleasing effect, by the contrast of these brilliant colors, especially when the surface is wet. This belt of metamorphic rock is seen to extend for a great distance to the north, giving a rounded outline to the summits in that direction, of which Mount Warren, about six miles distant and 13,000 feet high, as near as we could estimate, is one of the most prominent. The contrast between the contours of the metamorphic summits of the Sierra and the granitic ones will be seen on comparing Plates VII. and VIII.

Along the western and southern slopes of Mount Dana the traces of ancient glaciers are very distinct, up to a height of 12,000 feet. In the gap directly south of the summit a mass of ice must once have existed, having a thickness of at least 800 feet, at as high an elevation as 10,500 feet. From all the gaps and valleys of the west side of the range, tributary glaciers came down, and all united in one grand mass lower in the valley, where the medial moraines which accumulated between them are perfectly distinguishable, and in places as regularly formed as any to be seen in the Alps at the present day. On the eastern side of the pass, also, the traces of former glacial action are very marked, from the summit down to the foot of the cañon; and there are several small lakes which are of the kind known as "moraine lakes," formed by the damming up of the gorge by the terminal moraines left by the glacier as it melted away and retreated up the cañon.

Of the high peaks adjacent to Mount Dana, Mount Warren was ascended by Mr. Wackenreuder, and Mount Conness by Messrs. King and Gardner. The latter was reached by following a moraine which forms, as Mr. King remarks, a good graded road all the way round from Soda Springs to the very foot of the mountain. The ascent was difficult and somewhat hazardous, the approach to the summit being over a knife-blade ridge, which might be trying to the nerves of the uninitiated in mountain climbing. The summit is 12,692 feet above the sea-level, and is of granite, forming great concentric

Trail through talus on Duck Pass trail, July 1953.

plates dipping to the west. Of course, the view, like all from the dominant peaks of this region, is extensive, and grand beyond all description.

Our party also ascended the Mount Lyell fork, following up the valley of that stream. From near the head of it, the sketch was taken which is reproduced in Plate VIII. and which gives a good idea of the Alpine character of this portion of the Sierra. The highest point of the group was

Fig. 13.

SUMMIT OF MOUNT LYELL.

ascended by Messrs. Brewer and Hoffmann; but they were unable to reach the very summit, which was found to be a sharp and inaccessible pinnacle of granite rising above a field of snow. (See Fig. 13.) By observations taken at a station estimated to be 150 feet below the top of this pinnacle, Mount Lyell was found to be 13,217 feet high. The ascent was difficult, on account of the body of snow which had to be traversed, and which was softened by the sun, so that climbing in it was very laborious. This trouble might have been obviated, however, by camping nearer the summit and ascending before the sun had been up long enough to soften the snow. The culminating peaks of Mount Lyell have a gradual slope to the northeast; but to the south and southwest they break off in precipices a thousand feet or more in height. Between these cliffs, on that side, a vast amphitheatre is

32

included, once the birthplace of a grand glacier, which flowed down into the cañon of the Merced. From this point, the views of the continuation of the chain to the southeast are magnificent. Hundreds of points, in that direction, rise to an elevation of over 12,000 feet, mostly in jagged pinnacles of granite, towering above extensive snow-fields, with small plateaus between them. This continuation of the range to the southeast of Mount Lyell was afterwards visited by another party, and the peak called on the map Mount Ritter was ascended, as will be noticed farther on, after completing the tour around the Yosemite.

If the traveller has ascended Mount Dana, he will probably desire to return down the Tuolumne Valley and continue his journey on the trail leading south of Cloud's Rest, to the Little Yosemite and Sentinel Dome, and so back to Clark's Ranch. This trail strikes directly south from the crossing of the Tuolumne, a little below Soda Springs, and passes close under Cathedral Peak, on the west side, then along the back, or east side of Cloud's Rest, and down into the Little Yosemite Valley, as it is called.

This is a flat valley or mountain meadow, about four miles long and from half a mile to a mile wide. It is enclosed between walls from 2,000 to 3,000 feet high, with numerous projecting buttresses and angles, topped with dome-shaped masses. At the upper end of the valley it contracts to a V-shaped gorge, through which the Merced rushes with rapid descent, over huge masses of *débris*. The Little Yosemite Valley is a little over 6,000 feet above the sea-level, or 2,000 above the Yosemite, of which it is a kind of continuation, being on the same stream, — namely, the main Merced, — and only a short distance above the Nevada Fall, from the summit of which easy access may be had to it, whenever the bridge across the river between the Vernal and Nevada Falls has been rebuilt. This bridge, which was carried away in the winter of 1867 – 68, obviated the necessity of a very circuitous and difficult climb, to get from the base of the Nevada Fall to its summit, the ascent being quite easy on the north side of the river. On the south side, about midway up the Valley, a cascade comes sliding down in a clear sheet over a rounded mass of granite ; it was estimated at 1,200 feet in height. The concentric structure of the granite is beautifully marked in the Little Yosemite ; the curious rounded mass, called the Sugar Loaf, is a good instance of this.

The trail, leaving the Little Yosemite, crosses the divide between the Merced and the Illilouette, then the last-named stream, passing to the west of Mount Starr King, another of those remarkable conical knobs of granite, of which there is quite a group in this vicinity. From various points in the upper part of the Yosemite Valley, from which one can look up the Illilouette Cañon, the summit of Mount Starr King is just visible in the distance, nearly concealed behind another of these domes or cones, the two being with difficulty to be distinguished from each other, except when the sunlight happens to fall on one and not on the other, which is necessarily something of rather rare occurrence. Starr King is the steepest cone in the region, with the exception of the Half Dome, and is exceedingly smooth, having hardly a break in it; the summit is quite inaccessible, and we have not been able to measure its height.

There is nothing more of particular interest in this vicinity, nor before reaching Westfall's meadows, except the Sentinel Dome. This may be visited from Ostrander's, from which a trail has been blazed, or from the Illilouette Valley direct, on the return route. Horses may be ridden nearly to its summit, which is a great rounded mass of granite, with a few straggling pines on it. The view it commands is indeed sublime. Looking directly across the Yosemite, we have on the left the snow-covered mass of Mount Hoffmann, and, nearly under it, the rounded summit of the North Dome, and another similar mass of granite near it. In the centre of the field, the view extends directly up the Tenaya Cañon, past the stupendous vertical face of the Half Dome, on to the bare regular slope of Cloud's Rest, while on the opposite side of the cañon we see Mount Watkins, and, in the distance, the serrated crest of the Sierra. The points next to the left of Cloud's Rest, and directly over the Tenaya Cañon, belong to the Cathedral Peak and Unicorn Peak ranges, which are such prominent features in the view from Soda Springs. The tip of Cathedral Peak is just seen rising above the intervening ranges. Beyond, in the farthest distance, we have the higher range of Mount Conness and the adjacent peaks. The Half Dome is the great feature in this view, and no one can form any conception of its grandeur who has only seen it from the Valley below. On the Sentinel Dome we are 4,150 feet above the Valley; but still lack 587 feet of being as high as the summit of the Half Dome.

Facing the east, we have directly in front the Nevada Fall, with the Cap of Liberty on the left of it. Just above the latter we look into the Little Yosemite, and see a spot of its level floor, surrounded by bare, shelving granite masses. On the extreme left is a small portion of the bare side of the Half Dome, and the farthest point to the right is the Obelisk, or Mount Clark, the most western and dominating point of the Merced Group, its sides streaked with snow. In the extreme distance is the mass of mountains which we have called the Mount Lyell Group.*

Looking towards the southeast, we have a grand view of the whole of the Merced Group, in the distance, the Obelisk on the left, and the three other principal peaks to the right. Just midway between the Sentinel Dome and the Obelisk is the curious elevation called Mount Starr King, mentioned before as being an extremely steep, bare, inaccessible cone of granite, surrounded by several others of the same pattern, but of smaller dimensions.

The Sentinel Dome may easily be reached by the traveller to the Yosemite, by stopping over a day, on the way to or from the Valley, at Westfall's meadow. It makes just a pleasant day's excursion to ride to the Dome and back, with a few hours to remain on the summit. But if one is in a hurry, it is possible to make the trip and return in time to reach either Clark's or the Yosemite before night. To visit this region and not ascend Sentinel Dome, is a mistake; only those who have had the pleasure of making this excursion can appreciate how much is lost by not going there.

There is one point overhanging the Valley, about half a mile northeast of the Sentinel Dome, and directly in a line with the edge of the Half Dome. This is called Glacier Point, and the view from it combines perhaps more elements of beauty and grandeur than any other single one about the Valley. The Nevada and Vernal Falls are both plainly in sight, and directly over them is the Obelisk, with a portion of the range extending off to the right, until concealed behind the conical mass of Mount Starr King. To the left of the Cap of Liberty is the depression in which lies the Little Yosemite, and beyond this, in the farthest distance, the lofty summits of the Mount Lyell Group. The pines fringing the edge of Glacier Point are the *Pinus Jeffreyi*. The view of the Half Dome from this point is stupendous, as the

* Mount Lyell and Mount Maclure are two dark points visible to the right and the left of a snow-covered peak, rising in the farthest distance between the Nevada Fall and the Cap of Liberty.

spectator is very near to that object, and in a position to see it almost exactly edgewise. We regret that we are not able to give a figure of it from this point of view. Language is powerless to express the effect which this gigantic mass of rock, so utterly unlike anything else in the world, produces on the mind.

We have thus conducted the traveller around the Valley, and given him as many hints as our space will admit as to the character and locality of the objects to be seen on the route. A week is surely very little to devote to this excursion; and, when we consider how much can be seen and enjoyed during this time, it seems as if every one would be desirous of taking the opportunity of being at the Yosemite to make this addition to his travelling experience. The time will certainly come when this will be fully recognized, and when the rather indistinct trail around the Valley will be as well beaten as is now the one which leads into it.

For those who desire to extend their knowledge of the High Sierra still farther, there are numerous mountains, peaks, passes, and valleys to be visited, each one of which has its own peculiar beauties and attractions.

The Merced Group, which is so conspicuous an object in the view from Sentinel Dome and many other points about the Yosemite, offers a fine field for exploration. This group is a side-range, parallel with the main one, and about twelve miles from it. It runs from a point near the Little Yosemite, for about twelve miles, and then meets the transverse range coming from Mount Lyell and forming the divide between the San Joaquin and the Merced. Intersecting this, the Merced Group is continued to the southeast, and runs into a high peak, called Black Mountain; it then falls off, and becomes lost in the plateau which borders the San Joaquin.

At the northeast extremity of the group is the grand peak to which we first gave the name of the "Obelisk," from its peculiar shape, as seen from the region to the north of the Yosemite. It has, since that, been named Mount Clark, while the range to which it belongs is sometimes called the Obelisk Group, but, oftener, the Merced Group, because the branches of that river head around it. This is a noble range of mountains, with four conspicuous summits and many others of less prominence. The dominating peaks all lie at the intersection of spurs with the main range, as will be seen on the map. Mount Clark, or the Obelisk, is the one nearest the

36

Yosemite. All these peaks are nearly of the same height. The one next south of the Obelisk was called the Gray Peak, the next the Red Mountain, and the next Black Mountain, from the various colors which predominate on their upper portions. The last name had, however, been previously given to the highest point of the mass of ridges and peaks at the southern extremity of the range, south of the divide between the San Joaquin and the Merced. All these points, except Gray Peak, have been climbed by the Geological Survey, and they are all between 11,500 and 11,700 feet in elevation. Mount Clark was found to be an extremely sharp crest of granite, and was not climbed without considerable risk. Mr. King, who, with Mr. Gardner, made the ascent of the peak, says that its summit is so slender, that when on top of it they seemed to be suspended in the air.

An examination of the map will show how the spurs of the Merced Group break off in bold precipices to the north, with a more gradual descent to the south, — a peculiarity already mentioned as existing at the summit of Mount Hoffmann. The same is the case with the long crested ridge which forms the divide between the waters of the Merced and the San Joaquin. All these spurs and ridges open to the north with grand amphitheatres, where great glaciers once headed. The space enclosed between the Merced Group, the Mount Lyell Group, and the divide of the San Joaquin and Merced, forms a grand plateau about ten miles square, into which project the various spurs, coming down in parallel order, while in the centre there is a deep trough, sunk 2,000 feet below the general level, in which runs the Merced. The views from all the dominating points on the ridges surrounding this plateau are sublime, the region being one of the wildest and most inaccessible in the Sierra.

Our party, in charge of Mr. King, made an attempt to climb Mount Ritter, but, on account of the unfavorable weather, did not succeed in quite reaching the summit. They approached it from the southwest, passing to the south of Buena Vista Peak and Black Mountain. The Merced divide was found to be everywhere impassable for animals. Mr. King evidently considers Mount Ritter the culminating point of this portion of the Sierra, as he says that he climbed to a point about as high as Mount Dana, and had still above him an inaccessible peak some 400 or 500 feet high. To the south of this are some grand pinnacles of granite, very lofty and apparently inaccessible, to which we gave the name of "the Minarets." Our space is not sufficient to enable us to go into a description of this region; suffice it to say that there are here numerous peaks, yet unscaled and unnamed, to which the attention of mountain climbers is invited. Any one of them will furnish a panoramic view which will surely repay the lover of Alpine scenery for the expenditure of time and muscle required for its ascent.

There is a very interesting locality on the Tuolumne River, about sixteen miles from the Yosemite in a straight line, and in a direction a little west of north. It is called the Hetch-Hetchy Valley, an Indian name, the meaning of which we have been unable to ascertain. It is not only interesting on account of the beauty and grandeur of its scenery, but also because it is, in many respects, almost an exact counterpart of the Yosemite. It is not on quite so grand a scale as that valley; but, if there were no Yosemite, the Hetch-Hetchy would be fairly entitled to a world-wide fame; and, in spite of the superior attractions of the Yosemite, a visit to its counterpart may be recommended, if it be only to see how curiously Nature has repeated herself.

The Hetch-Hetchy may be reached easily from Big Oak Flat, by taking the regular Yosemite trail, by Sprague's ranch and Big Flume, as far as Mr. Hardin's fence, between the south and middle forks of the Tuolumne River. Here, at a distance of about eighteen miles from Big Oak Flat, the trail turns off to the left, going to Wade's meadows, or Big Meadows as they are also called, the distance being about seven miles. From Wade's ranch the trail crosses the middle fork of the Tuolumne, and goes to the "Hog ranch," a distance of five miles, then up the divide between the middle fork and the main river, to another little ranch called "the Cañon." From here, it winds down among the rocks for six miles, to the Hetch-Hetchy, or the Tuolumne Cañon. This trail was made by Mr. Joseph Screech, and is well blazed, and has been used for driving sheep and cattle into the Valley. The whole distance from Big Oak Flat is called thirty-eight miles. Mr. Screech first visited this place in 1850, at which time the Indians had possession. The Pah Utes still visit it every year for the purpose of getting the acorns, having driven out the western slope Indians, just as they did from the Yosemite.

The Hetch-Hetchy is between 3,800 and 3,900 feet above the sea-level, or nearly the same as the Yosemite; it is three miles long east and west,

Inviting, wild backcountry deep in the Sierra.

but is divided into two parts by a spur of granite, which nearly closes it up in the centre. The portion of the Valley below this spur is a large open meadow, a mile in length, and from an eighth to half a mile in width, with excellent grass, timbered only along, the edge. The meadow terminates below in an extremely narrow cañon, through which the river has not sufficient room to flow at the time of the spring freshets, so that the Valley is then inundated, giving rise to a fine lake. The upper part of the Valley, east of the spur, is a mile and three quarters long, and from an eighth to a third of a mile wide, well timbered and grassed. The walls of this Valley are not quite so high as those of the Yosemite; but still, anywhere else than in California, they would be considered as wonderfully grand. On the north side of the Hetch-Hetchy is a perpendicular bluff, the edge of which is 1,800 feet above the Valley, and having a remarkable resemblance to El Capitan. In the spring, when the snows are melting, a large stream is precipitated over this cliff, falling at least 1,000 feet perpendicular. The volume of water is very large, and the whole of the lower part of the Valley is said to be filled with its spray.

A little farther east is the Hetch-Hetchy Fall, the counterpart of the Yosemite. The height is 1,700 feet. It is not quite perpendicular; but it comes down in a series of beautiful cascades, over a steeply-inclined face of rock. The volume of water is much larger than that of the Yosemite Fall, and, in the spring, its noise can be heard for miles. The position of this fall in relation to the Valley is exactly like that of the Yosemite Fall in its Valley, and opposite to it is a rock much resembling the Cathedral Rock, and 2,270 feet high.

At the upper end of the Valley the river forks, one branch, nearly as large as the main river, coming in from near Castle Peak. Above this, the cañon, so far as we know, is unexplored; but, in all probability, has concealed in it some grand falls. There is no doubt that the great glacier, which, as already mentioned, originated near Mount Dana and Mount Lyell, found its way down the Tuolumne Cañon, and passed through the Hetch-Hetchy Valley. How far beyond this it reached we are unable to say, for we have made no explorations in the cañon below. Within the Valley, the rocks are beautifully polished, up to at least 800 feet above the river. Indeed, it is probable that the glacier was much thicker than this; for, along, the trail, near the south

40

end of the Hetch-Hetchy, a moraine was observed at the elevation of fully 1,200 feet above the bottom of the Valley. The great size and elevation of the amphitheatre in which the Tuolumne glacier headed caused such an immense mass of ice to be formed that it descended far below the line of perpetual snow before it melted away. The plateau, or amphitheatre, at the head of the Merced was not high enough to allow a glacier to be formed of sufficient thickness to descend down as far as into the Yosemite Valley; at least, we have obtained no positive evidence that such was the case. The statement to that effect in the " Geology of California," Vol. I., is an error, although it is certain that the masses of ice approached very near to the edge of the Valley, and were very thick in the cañon to the southeast of Cloud's Rest, and on down into the Little Yosemite.

This chapter may be closed by adding a few pages in regard to a portion of the High Sierra beyond the limits of the map accompanying this volume, but to which we desire to direct attention, as including the loftiest and the grandest mountains, and the most stupendous mountain scenery, yet discovered within our own territory.

By referring to the Table on page 39, it will be observed that between latitudes 36° and 37° there are peaks and passes higher than those described as existing near the Yosemite, there being a general rise of the mass of the Sierra as we go south. This high region, in which the passes exceed 12,000, and the peaks rise, in one instance at least, to 15,000 feet, lies at the head of King's and Kern Rivers and the San Joaquin. The most elevated peaks are between the parallels of 36° 30′ and 37°, and are distant from the Yosemite, in a southeast direction, from 90 to 110 miles. This region was first explored by the Geological Survey in 1864, and a synopsis of the results of this reconnoissance will be found in the " Geology of California," Vol. I. (pp. 365 – 402), from which some extracts will here be introduced, in the hope of attracting the attention of some travellers, who may thus be induced to push their explorations beyond the comparatively narrow limits of a trip to and around the Yosemite. The region in question is not very difficult of access; indeed, a very good idea of its grandeur may be obtained by only a short trip from Visalia and back.

Our party, consisting of Messrs. Brewer, Hoffmann, King, Gardner, and Cotter, took the field in May and proceeded from San Francisco across the plains of the San Joaquin to Visalia, from which point they entered the Sierra, ascending King's River to its source, and exploring the whole region about the head-waters of that and Kern River. Thence they made their way across the range by a pass over 12,000 feet high, passed up Owen's Valley, ascended the west branch of Owen's River, crossing the Sierra again at an altitude of 12,400 feet, and thence descending to the head of the San Joaquin River. The exploration was continued through the region of the head-waters of that stream and the Merced, connecting the reconnoissance with that of 1863 around the sources of the Tuolumne. The whole expedition occupied about three months, during which time the geography and geology of a district including an area of over 10,000 square miles were for the first time explored, the whole region having previously been entirely unknown. The results proved to be of the greatest interest, disclosing the fact that this was the highest part of the Sierra Nevada, which was something quite unexpected to most persons, Mount Shasta having long been considered the most elevated point in California.

Thomas's Saw-mill (Camp 164), at an elevation of 5,484 feet above the sea, and about forty miles northeast of Visalia, may be made the base of supplies for an expedition to this region. The mill stands on the edge of a beautiful meadow, the water from which runs into King's River. It is surrounded by a magnificent forest of the usual coniferous trees found in the Sierra at this altitude, and a little higher up the Big Trees (*Sequoia gigantea*) are abundant, as will be noticed in the next chapter.

A rocky summit, called Bald Mountain, about six miles east of Thomas's Mill, was ascended by our party for the purpose of getting the first idea of the topography of the unknown region about to be visited. It is easy of access, although 7,936 feet high, and offers a fine view of the neighboring country and the extended crest of the Sierra. Its position is at once seen to be on the great elevated divide between the waters of King's River on the north, and the Kaweah on the south. This divide runs up to the snowy mountains at the summit of the chain, and appeared to terminate in the highest group of peaks, some twenty-five or thirty miles distant. The ridge of the divide rises at intervals into peaks, each one commanding the country on either side and behind it, as well as forward to the east as far as the next high point in that direction. About eight or nine miles to the north,

42

The weather threatens over a backcountry lake in the Sierra Nevada. Professor Whitney describes the varied Sierra scenes as having both "gloom and glory". This landscape is one of gloom. An hour after this photo was taken a driving blizzard drove the backpack party to a lower altitude.

and several thousand feet below, is the cañon of King's River, which seems precipitous and impassable. Some twenty miles to the northeast this river divides into two branches, and the course of the northern of these is such that the observer on the summit of Bald Mountain can look directly into it. The view is most impressive. Granite walls with buttresses, pinnacles, and domes rise perpendicularly from three to five thousand feet above the river, and above these the bare, rocky slopes tower up, high above all vegetation into regions of perpetual snow. Dark lines of trees wind up the ravines on the mountain-sides, becoming thinner and more scattered, until they disappear altogether, the summits of the mountains rising far above all vegetation, barren and desolate.

Such is the character of the divide between the main forks of the King's River, although the southern side is not as steep as the northern. Its lofty summit, everywhere crested with precipices, presented an insurmountable barrier, over which our party never succeeded in taking their animals. Just at the junction of the forks, the end of the divide is crossed by a broad red stripe, bearing about northwest, and which could be seen appearing again on the north side of the cañon. This, which seemed to be a great dyke of volcanic rock, but which was afterwards found to be a vein of granite, led to giving the divide the name of "Dyke Ridge."

An attempt was first made to reach the summit of the Sierra by travelling up this divide, an old Indian trail being discovered which was followed for about fifteen miles. This trail led to a point where the ridge widened out into a plateau occupied by a large meadow; a number of cattle had been driven here, and the place was known to hunters as the "Big Meadows." Camp 165 was intermediate between Thomas's and the Big Meadows, and was 7,480 feet above the sea. The rock along the whole route is granite, which has a tendency to weather into grand, rounded, boulder-like masses. Camp 166, about two miles below the Big Meadows, but nearly at the same altitude, was at an elevation of 7,827 feet. Here the massive granite is traversed by occasional dykes of a fine-grained variety of the same rock, and with veins of milky quartz. Large areas of nearly level or gently-sloping ground occur here, covered with meadows or forests of *Pinus contorta*, and there are also extensive patches of bare rock, or of granitic sand derived from its decomposition. As the granite decomposes very irregularly, the

44

harder portions rise in rocky, rounded hills, and the softer are occupied by small valleys. A series of these grassy plats, five or six miles in length, makes up the Big Meadows, and they are drained in both directions, namely, into the King's and Kaweah Rivers. At this altitude the sugar and pitch pines, as well as the Big Trees, are left behind, and the forests are made up of the dark and sombre fir and *Pinus contorta*. Although it was the month of June, the thermometer sank as low as 16° at night, and a snow-storm, of three or four hours' duration occurred.

Just east of the Big Meadows, and on the summit of the divide, are two elevations, to which the name of "Dome Mountains" was given, from the finely rounded, dome-like sweep of their outlines, which contrasts in a striking manner with the sharpness of the summit peaks behind them. On their southern sides the forests rise in an unbroken curve to their summits; but on the north side there is a precipice for 200 to 300 feet below the crest, then a short, concave curve, and then the rounded and wooded slope descending to the King's River Valley. In this part of the mountains, as at the Yosemite, the granite exhibits a tendency to form dome-shaped masses on a grand scale; but on the very crest or summit-range it rises in pinnacles, giving a very different character to the scenery, as will be noticed further on. That one of these Dome Mountains which was ascended was found to be 9,825 feet high. Its summit was made up of concentric layers or beds of granite, from one to five feet thick, breaking into large rectangular masses sufficiently smooth and regular in form to be used for masonry without dressing. The north slope of the mountain is covered by immense masses of this angular *débris*. That this concentric structure is not the result of the original stratification of the rock, is evident from a study of the phenomena, which do not indicate anything like anticlinal or synclinal axes, or any irregular folding. The curves are arranged strictly with reference to the surface of the masses of rock, showing clearly that they must have been produced by the contraction of the material while cooling or solidifying, and also giving very strongly the impression that, in many places, we see something of the original shape of the surface, as it was when the granitic mass assumed its present position. In the cañons between these domes, we sometimes have large surfaces exposed by denudation, and, as a result of the original concentric structure of the rocks on each side, we see the great

45

plates of granite overlapping each other, and where considerable weathering and denudation has taken place, we have picturesque and curious forms as the result; pyramids and pinnacles are left standing on the prominent points, and their bedded structure adds to the peculiar impression which they give of their being works of art rather than of nature. Fig. 14 will serve to illustrate the kind of scenery which is common in the region of this concentrically bedded granite.

Fig. 14.

GRANITE ROCKS NEAR CAMP 169.

The route followed by the party, in their attempt to reach the summit, led around the north side of the Domes, over the huge piles of angular fragments, and was on this account tedious and difficult. Camp 167 was made at a point two miles northeast of the Dome, and at an altitude of 8,890 feet above the sea. Camp 168 was four or five miles southeast of the Dome, at a small meadow on the divide, and at an elevation of 9,569 feet. Progress was necessarily very slow, owing to the heavy load of provisions and instruments with which the small train of animals was packed, and the extreme roughness of the region travelled over. Beyond the Domes the

46

The John Muir Trail frequently leads the hiker through dense, sweetly-pungent forested areas such as this one on the trail to Virginia Lake.

divide contracts to a mere ridge; the slope to the south, although steep, is comparatively smooth, and spreads out, towards its base, into rolling wooded spurs, between which small brooks run down into the Kaweah. Nearly all these streams head in little sedgy meadows, whose bright green contrasts beautifully with the deep shade of the surrounding forests. To the north, the aspect of things was different; instead of a smooth slope, there was a fractured granite precipice, descending 200 feet, then a slope of *débris*, and at its foot two small lakes, forming the head-waters of a stream which unites with the south fork of King's River, a few miles above the dyke. This stream was called Glacier Brook, from the abundant traces of former glacial action in its vicinity. From Camp 168 to the Big Meadows is only sixteen miles; but so difficult was the way, that it required two days for the party to accomplish that distance. From this camp, and the next (No. 169), two miles farther up the divide, an examination was made of an interesting and characteristic feature in the topography of this granitic region, and to which the name of "The Kettle" was given.

This is a rocky amphitheatre at the head of a stream which flows back directly northeast from its source towards the axis of the chain, for a distance of twelve miles, and then curves and enters King's River, a peculiar and almost unique course for a stream in the Sierra Nevada. The kettle-like form of the head of this valley may be seen from the annexed section across

Fig. 15.

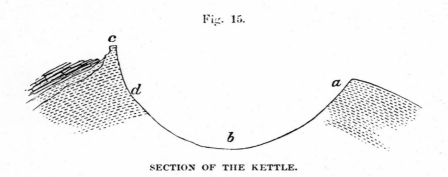

SECTION OF THE KETTLE.

it transversely, at a distance of about a mile from its head (Fig. 15); it is plotted on an equal scale of horizontal and vertical distances.

The northern rim (*a*) is about 1,100 feet above the bottom (*b*); the southern one (*c*) rises in a sharp ridge 1,606 feet above *b*; in some places *c d* is a vertical wall, in others a steep slope. The distance from *a* to *c* is a

48

little less than a mile. The Kettle is open at the north-northeast end, and extends as a green valley some six miles, to the south fork of King's River. There are several small domes and pinnacles on the east side, and in some places the granite along the rim forms a parapet, which has a striking resemblance to an artificial structure, as the rock is most beautifully and regularly bedded, so that the wall seems to vie with the most finished mason-work in execution. The annexed woodcut (Fig. 16) will show the exact appearance of a portion of this wall, which is in some places so thin that the light can be seen shining through between the cracks. It is from eight to twenty feet high.

Fig. 16.

RIM OF THE KETTLE.

This rim of the Kettle is a beautiful illustration of the concentric or "dome-structure" of the granite of this region. The dotted lines in Fig. 15 show the bedding or lamination of the rock, in the cross-section of the whole, and Fig. 17 explains how the parapet has been formed by the wearing away of a part of the concentrically-laminated granite near the summit. This peculiar crater-like cavity in the granite is typical of many others seen afterwards in this region, the origin of which it seems impossible to refer to any ordinary denudation, or to the action of glaciers. These cavities were

49

all occupied by masses of ice, as is evident from the polish of the interior walls and bottom of each of them; but it hardly needs to be added that no glacial action could have originally formed one of these kettles; the most that it could do would be to scour out and polish up the interior. This subject will be discussed in the second volume of the "Geology of California."

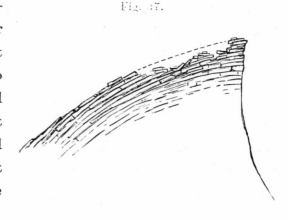

Fig. 17.

Beyond the Kettle the divide becomes quite impassable for animals, and nearly so for men. Several unsuccessful trials were made to pass the barrier of nearly perpendicular rocks; but, at last, a chink in the granite was found, through which the party crawled, and proceeded to ascend the next high peak on the divide, which is about six miles southeast of Camp 169, the elevation of which was found to be 11,623 feet above the sea. From its summit a magnificent view was obtained of the crest of the Sierra, as well as of the divide which had been traversed by the party. The region to the east presented a complicated system of very sharp ridges, rising here and there into pinnacles, apparently all of granite, with numerous immense circular amphitheatral cavities, formed by sharp ridges surrounding basins, of which one side is always broken away, and which have exactly the appearance of ancient craters both in form and outline. To the west the predominance of rounded or dome-shaped mountain summits was most striking, the whole country appearing as if it had suddenly been cooled or congealed while violently boiling.

Camp 170 was about seven miles north-northeast of No. 169, in the valley of the stream which flows from the Kettle, and at an altitude of 7,408 feet, which was a lower point than was afterwards reached by the party for a long time. The way to this camp led around the west and north sides of the Kettle over a region exceedingly difficult to traverse, with alternating steep, naked slopes of granite, and thick, low forests. Some of the ancient moraines, piles of angular fragments of granite, were almost insurmountable obstacles to the passage of the animals. This camp was situated behind a sharp granite knob which rises from the valley like a sugar-loaf, as seen from below; but

A day's trek away from the roadhead will bring the hiker to areas that are devoid of crowds—beautiful backcountry, that may be enjoyed in its relatively pristine state. This hiking party is starting the ascent out of Cascade Valley.

which, in reality, is the end of a ridge a mile or two in length. This is several hundred feet high, and its summit is quite inaccessible. Its sides show undoubted evidence that it was once surrounded by a great glacier flowing down the valley. The slopes directed towards the moving ice are worn and polished, and huge boulders have been pushed up on them, and left all along, wherever the angle was not too steep for fragments of rock to lie. The meadow occupies a basin behind this knob, which appears to have been scooped out by a glacier.

From the Sugar Loaf Rock there is a magnificent view up the valley to the group of mountains forming the western crest of the Sierra, the culminating point of which was named Mount Brewer. This was directly east, and about ten miles distant. A grand view was also had of the great moraine on the eastern side of the extreme south fork of King's River; this moraine stretches along for six or eight miles in an unbroken line, resembling an immense artificial embankment. There is another one on the opposite side of the valley which is also very distinct, but the eastern one is much the larger. The horizontal distance across from one to the other is about a mile and a half. At a distance these moraines appear as regular as railroad embankments, their crests being quite smooth, and having a uniform and gradual inclination up the valley. To ascend or descend their sides with animals, is a task of considerable difficulty; but, once on the top, travelling is quite easy. In the bottom of the valley the granite is everywhere grooved and beautifully polished.

The view of the cañon, towards its head, as seen from this moraine, near Camp 175, was sublime, strongly resembling the valley of the Yosemite in some of its grandest features. It curves but little, so that the view is unobstructed. Great surfaces and precipices of naked granite are seen, often over 1,000 feet high, but seldom vertical, although sloping at a very high angle; these surfaces are everywhere in the valley rounded and polished. Side cañons of the same character, but still more precipitous, open into the main one.

From Camp 171, Mount Brewer was twice ascended, on the 2d and 4th of July, by passing up the valley in which the camp was situated, and which divides at the base of the mountain, extending up to the crest of the ridge. Its sides were found to be very steep up to above 12,000 feet, the southern one being an almost vertical wall of 1,000 feet in height. The granite of this region is hard, not very coarse, and of a light ash-gray color, with a pearly lustre when seen in great masses. It is intersected with veins

MOUNT BREWER, FROM A POINT THREE MILES DISTANT, LOOKING EAST.

of quartz and also of feldspar, and with some made up of a mixture of both these minerals; these veins were rarely more than two or three feet in thickness. In general, however, the rock is remarkably homogeneous and almost destitute of accidental minerals, a little epidote being the only one observed in this region.

The view from the summit of Mount Brewer is one of the most sublime which it is possible to obtain, even in this sublimest portion of the Sierra. The snowy peaks, rising to over 11,000 feet in elevation, cover a breadth of more than twenty-five miles, and the point of view on the summit of this mountain is such, that the observer is placed in the very midst of this grand assemblage. High peaks, sharp ridges bristling with pinnacles, rocky amphitheatres, and deep cañons constitute the main features of the scene. The summit is a loose and shattered mass of angular pieces of granite, forming a ridge some thirty feet long by five broad, which from the west appears as a sharp cone. The eastern side of the mountain is a precipice buttressed by a thin ridge, running out between two great vertically-walled basins, white with snow, which contrasts beautifully with the vivid blue of the frozen lakes 3,000 feet below.

The barometrical measurements make the height of Mount Brewer 13,886 feet; it is not, however, the culminating point of the Sierra, but is on a spur embraced by two branches of King's River. Ten miles farther east another ridge stretches in an unbroken line north and south, and through its depressions the blue ranges of the desert are plainly seen. On this ridge there are fourteen peaks visible, ten of which are as high as Mount Brewer, and four higher. One of these, directly opposite, and which appeared to be the highest point but one, was called Mount Tyndall, in honor of this distinguished physicist and Alpine explorer. The other high point, eight miles south of Mount Tyndall, and, so far as known, the culminating peak of the Sierra, was named by the party Mount Whitney. Farther observations, by Mr. King, showed that a point about two miles northeast of Mount Tyndall was a little higher than this mountain; it was named in honor of Major R. S. Williamson, of the United States Engineers, so well known by his topographical labors on the Pacific coast, especially in connection with the United States railroad surveys. Thirty-two miles north-northwest is a very high mountain, called Mount Goddard, in honor of a Civil Engineer who has done much to advance our knowledge of the geography of California, and who is the author of "Britton and Rey's Map." A transverse ridge running obliquely across from Mount Brewer to Mount Tyndall forms the divide between the head-waters of the Kern and those of King's River. South of this, the division of the summit of the Sierra into two parallel ridges is very marked, the Kern flowing in the tremendous gorge between

54

Headin' for Tully's Hole and base camp.

them. The eastern ridge forms an almost unbroken wall for a great distance to the north, while the western one is less distinctly marked, being broken through to allow of the passage of the head-waters of the King's and San Joaquin Rivers. The highest portion of the western ridge is that extending between Mount Brewer and Kaweah Peak, twelve miles to the south. This last-named peak was not reached by our party, but its height was estimated to be over 14,000 feet. From its great elevation and peculiar position, opposite to the highest point of the Sierra, and the immense depth of the cañon of the Kern between it and Mount Whitney, it would probably command the grandest view which could be obtained in the whole range of the Sierra. Kaweah Peak is distinctly visible from Visalia, to one looking up the valley of the Kaweah River.

Of the terrible grandeur of the region embraced in this portion of the Sierra it is hardly possible to convey any idea. Mr. Gardner, in his notes of the view from Mount Brewer, thus enumerates some of the most striking features of the scene: "Cañons from two to five thousand feet deep, between thin ridges topped with pinnacles sharp as needles; successions of great, crater-like amphitheatres, with crowning precipices over sweeping snow-fields and frozen lakes; everywhere naked and shattered granite without a sign of vegetation, except where a few gnarled and storm-beaten pines (*Pinus contorta*, *P. albicaulis*, and *P. aristata*) cling to the rocks in the deeper cañons; such were the elements of the scene we looked down upon, while cold gray clouds were drifting overhead."

The upper part of the mountain slopes rapidly on all sides for 2,000 feet from the summit, then falls off more gradually on the west towards the cañon of the south fork of King's River. On the east, it breaks off suddenly into a great amphitheatre, the head of a cañon between 4,000 and 5,000 feet deep below the crest, surrounded by sheer vertical walls, and with glacier-polished slopes at the bottom, over which are scattered several small and beautiful lakes. These cañons and precipices, which lie between the two principal ridges, constitute the main difficulty in reaching and exploring the eastern summit peaks. The region is desolate and cold; but these hindrances, incidental to all high mountain climbing, could be overcome, were it not for the impassable precipices which continually block the way, necessitating long *détours*, and rendering it impossible to reach any high

56

peak without a long series of perilous and extremely fatiguing ascents and descents.

As want of provisions and the absolute impossibility of proceeding any farther with the animals were sufficient reasons to prevent the whole party from making any attempt to climb the summit of the eastern ridge, Mr. King volunteered to undertake this task, although it seemed to most of the party that it was quite impossible to reach either of the highest peaks from the western side. Packing provisions for six days and one blanket, he started, accompanied by Richard Cotter, from the camp at the base of Mount Brewer, July 4th, and •the following account of the trip, in which the summit of Mount Tyndall was reached, is given nearly in Mr. King's own words : —

"To follow down the ridge which forms the divide between King's and Kern Rivers, and which runs obliquely across from Mount Brewer to Mount Tyndall, was impossible, for it rose in sharp crags above us, and had we been able to pass around these, we should have been stopped by vertical clefts over a thousand feet deep. We began, therefore, to climb down the eastern slope of the ridge, instead of trying to keep on its crest. The only way down was along a sloping shelf, on which we were obliged to proceed with the greatest caution, as our packs had a constant tendency to over-balance us, and a single misstep would have been fatal. At last we reached the base of the cliff safely, and made our way rapidly down a long snow-slope and over huge angular masses of *débris* to the margin of a frozen lake.

"We were now in the amphitheatre; the crags towering around us were all inaccessible, and we were obliged to spend six hours in climbing down from the outlet of the lake, over a slope of smooth granite, polished by glaciers and kept constantly wet by a shallow current of water, into King's River cañon, and then up again over a long, difficult *débris* slope and across several fields of snow, into another amphitheatre. Of this the southern wall is the divide between King's and Kern Rivers. The sky by this time had become quite overcast, and we were obliged to take refuge under some over-hanging rocks, while a severe hail-storm went by. We started on again, hoping to cross over to Kern Cañon; but the ascent proved very difficult, and night overtook us at the foot of a cliff 2,000 feet high. There was no wood, so we burned paper and dead carices enough to make some lukewarm tea, and finding a crevice among the ice and granite blocks, somewhat sheltered from the biting winds, we retired. The elevation was over 12,000 feet, and the air stinging cold; but the sunset view was glorious. The east wall of the basin was brilliantly lighted up, its hundred pinnacles were of pure yellow, relieved by the dark blue of the sky, which is so noticeable when one looks up from a deep cañon in the Sierra. A long slope of snow opposite us warmed with a soft rosy tinge (the Alpine glow), and the rugged ridge behind us cast a serrated gray shadow across it, which slowly crept up and scaled the granite wall, until only the very topmost spires were in the light. All night long, large masses of granite came crashing down from the crags overhead, striking at times too near for comfort.

"The next morning we ate our frozen venison by starlight, and started at sunrise to ascend the snow-slope before it should become softened. We had to cut steps, and after working up awhile it became quite difficult, so that we were three hours in reaching the rocks, after which we climbed two hours more, until we came to a very bad ravine where it was impossible to proceed with our packs. It was now that our reata came into play, and we took turns in climbing the length of it, and pulling packs and blankets after us, reaching the top about noon, by which time the novelty of this method of ascent had quite worn off. What was our consternation to find ourselves, as we scaled the summit, on the brink of an almost Yosemite cliff! We walked along the edge, however, for some distance, until at last we discovered three shelves, each about fifty feet below the other, from the lowest of which we might, by good luck and hard climbing, work along the face of the cliff to a sort of ravine, down which we might probably reach the *débris*. I tied the reata firmly about my body, and Cotter lowered me down to the first shelf; he then carefully sent down the precious barometer and our packs. Next, he made a fast loop in the lasso, hooked it over a point of rock and came down hand over hand, whipping the rope off the rock to which it had been fastened, thus severing our communication with the top of the cliff. This operation was repeated, not without considerable danger, from the impossibility of finding a firm rock around which to secure the rope, until the bottom was at last safely reached. At the foot of the *débris* was a beautiful lake half a mile long, once the bottom of the bed of a glacier.

"There were a few *Pinus contorta* visible down the course of the Kern, — here only a small brook, — and quite a grove of *P. aristata*; these, with a few willows and an Alpine *Ribes*, were all the vegetation we could see, excepting a few carices. Camp was made at the base of the peak, after climbing up a difficult ridge, near a little cluster of the *Pinus contorta*; this was about 11,000 feet above the sea.

"The next day the summit was reached, without serious difficulty, after some risky climbing of smooth dome-shaped masses of granite, where the only support and aid in climbing was an occasional crack. The barometer stood, at 12 M., at 18,104, the temperature of the air being 44°. On setting the level, it was seen at once that there were two peaks equally high in sight, and two still more elevated, all within a distance of seven miles. Of the two highest, one rose close by, hardly a mile away; it is an inaccessible bunch of needles, and we gave it the name of Mount Williamson. The other, which we called Mount Whitney, appeared equally inaccessible from any point on the north or west side; it is between seven and eight miles distant, in a south-southeast direction, and I should think fully 350 feet higher than our peak. (Farther examination showed that it was really 600 or 700 feet higher than Mount Tyndall.) Within our field of view were five mountains over 14,000 feet, and about fifty peaks over 13,000.

"The five highest peaks are all on the eastern ridge. Owen's Valley, a brown sage plain, lies 10,000 feet below on the one side, and Kern Cañon, once the rocky bed of a grand old glacier, 4,000 feet down on the other. About fifteen miles north of here, King's River cuts through the western ridge and turns at a right angle towards the plain. North of this point, again, the two great ridges unite in a grand pile of granite mountains, whose outlines are all of the most rugged and fantastic character. Twenty-five miles south, the high group ends, there (certainly for a breadth of sixty miles) forming one broad, rolling, forest-covered plateau, 8,000 to 9,000 feet in elevation.

"From Mount Brewer to Kaweah Peak, the two culminating points of the western ridge, for a distance of fifteen miles, there is nothing that can be called a separate mountain; it is, rather, a great mural ridge, capped by small, sharp cones and low, ragged domes, all covered with little minarets. At one place the ridge forms a level table; upon this lies an unbroken cover of snow. To the eastward, all this range, from King's River gateway to Kaweah Peak, presents a series of blank, almost perpendicular precipices, broken every mile or so by a bold granite buttress. Between these are vast snow-fields, and also numberless deep lakes, of which the most elevated are frozen."

The elevation of Mount Tyndall, as calculated from Mr. King's observations, compared with those of the other party, and with the station barometer at Visalia, was fixed at 14,386 feet; this is only fifty-four feet less than the altitude of Mount Shasta.

After Mr. King's return to Camp 171, at the eastern base of Mount Brewer, the whole party went back to Big Meadows, having been out of provisions for several days, with the exception of a few strips of jerked bear meat. Here, also, they were to meet the escort which was considered indispensable for safely exploring the region to the north. Mr. King, however, not being satisfied with his first attempt to reach the culminating point of the Sierra, made another start from Visalia July 14th, with no other company than an escort of two soldiers. His intention was to follow the Owen's Lake and Visalia trail, which leads up the Kaweah River, keeping the south fork from its junction with the main river. It was supposed that it might be possible to reach the summit of Mount Whitney from this side, previous explorations having shown that this could not be accomplished from the northwest or west.

The first camp was at forty miles distance from the edge of the foot-hills, the road up the valley being intensely hot, dry, and dusty. From this camp the trail led over a rolling plateau of high altitude (probably between 8,000 and 9,000 feet), partly covered by forests of *Pinus contorta*, and partly by chains of meadows. North of the road was a range of bald, granite hills, with groves of pine scattered about their bases, an occasional patch of snow appearing on the higher points. This chain of peaks seems to be the continuation of the divide between the south and main Kaweah Rivers, and it continues eastward to the summit of the Sierra, being the southern termination of the high ranges to the north; south of it the country falls off gradually to Walker's Pass, forming numerous broad, flat-topped ridges, which give the region the general aspect of a table-land, scored down from north to south by parallel cañons, of which the Kern occupies the deepest. The main and north forks of this river rise far to the north of this table-land, and cut their way through it, while the south fork heads on its southern slope, and joins the main river, about eight miles below where the trail crosses. This plateau is entirely of granite, and the vegetation varies according to the altitude. West of the cañon of the south fork, the forests are chiefly of the *Pinus contorta;* between this and the main Kern are fine groves of *P. Jeffreyi,* and occasional oaks. Where the trail crosses the main Kern, the river is twenty-five or thirty yards wide; the water is clear and cold, and abundantly supplied with trout.

From this point the old trail bent southward, crossing the mountains some distance below Little Owen's Lake; the new one was built no farther, and from here it was necessary to continue the exploration, without any other guides than the eye and the compass. Striking the north fork of the Kern, at that point only a brook four or five yards wide, Mr. King followed it up for several miles, to where it breaks through an east and west range of craggy peaks, which comes down like an immense spur, at right-angles to the general course of the Sierra, and is continued as an elevated ridge far down the north side of the Kaweah. This range heads in a very high and bare granitic peak, called Sheep Rock, from the great number of mountain sheep found in this vicinity. It is about eight miles south of Mount Whitney, and is the termination of this high portion of the Sierra.

North of this spur or lateral range through which the north and main forks of the Kern both make their way, there is a quadrilateral area, comprised between the two great divisions of the Sierra on the east and west sides, and having on the north the transverse ridge which connects Mount Tyndall with Mount Whitney. In this the main Kern heads with many branches, and to the east of it, in the midst of every difficulty, Mr. King worked for three days before he could reach the base of the mountain, whose summit he was endeavoring to attain. All his efforts, however, proved unsuccessful, so far as this particular object was concerned; but he was enabled to determine the main features of the topography of a considerable area, which otherwise would necessarily have been left an entire blank upon our map. The highest point reached by him was, according to the most reliable calculations, 14,740 feet above the sea-level. At the place where this observation was taken he was, as near as he was able to estimate, between 300 and 400 feet lower than the culminating point of the mountain, which must, therefore, somewhat exceed 15,000 feet in height.

The summit is a ridge having somewhat the outline of a helmet, the perpendicular face being turned towards the east, and there is snow on its summit, which indicates that there must be a flat surface there. It is the culminating point of an immense pile of granite, which is cut almost to the centre by numerous steep and often almost vertical cañons, ending in high-walled amphitheatres. Southward of the main peak there is a range of sharp needles, four of which are over 14,000 feet high. The general aspect of the group is much like that of Mount Tyndall. Mount Whitney has been approached on all sides, except from the east, and, so far, found to be utterly inaccessible.

During the time while Mr. King was exploring about the sources of Kern River, Professor Brewer and party continued their route northward, in the hope of being able to cross over the higher ridges of the Sierra to the head of the San Joaquin. They left the Big Meadows and made their way into the great cañon of the south fork of King's River by a terribly steep road, the descent being between 4,500 and 5,000 feet. The cañon here is very much like the Yosemite. It is a valley, from half a mile to a mile wide at the bottom, about eleven miles long, and closed at the lower end by a deep and inaccessible ravine like that below the Yosemite, but deeper and more precipitous. It expands above and branches at its head, and is everywhere surrounded and walled in by grand precipices, broken here and there by side cañons, resembling the Yosemite in its main features. The walls of the King's River cañon, however, are nowhere vertical to so great a height as El Capitan; but rather resemble the Sentinel and Cathedral Rocks, or the Three Brothers, of the Yosemite Valley. They rise at various points to heights estimated to be from 3,500 to 6,000 feet above their base, and there is but little *débris* at the foot of the walls. The height of the lower end of the valley above the sea was found to be approximately 4,737 feet; that of the upper end, 5,218 feet. At the head of the valley, occupying a position analogous to that of the Half Dome at the Yosemite, is the most elevated part of the wall; it is nearly vertical, and between 6,500 and 7,000 feet high.

The King's River cañon rivals and even surpasses the Yosemite Valley in

62

the altitude of its surrounding cliffs; but it has no features so striking as the Half Dome, or Tutucanula, nor has it the stupendous waterfalls which make that valley quite unrivalled in beauty; its streams descend by a series of what may be called (in California) cascades, of from 150 to 200 feet high.

The bottom of the valley is covered with granitic sand, forming a soil which supports a fine growth of timber, with here and there a meadow. The river abounds in trout.

The party came into the valley by an old Indian foot-trail, which passes out by the north fork, over an exceedingly rough country, and must cross the Sierra at an elevation of at least 13,000 feet. This trail was entirely impracticable for animals. As it was quite impossible to get north at the head of the valley, the party returned a distance of two or three miles, and made their way out on the north side, by an exceedingly steep and difficult route, camping four or five miles from the edge of the cañon, and at an elevation of more than 4,000 feet above it, or 9,308 feet above the sea. This camp (No. 180) was situated between the two main forks of King's River, and from it a series of fruitless attempts were made to reach Mount Goddard, about twenty-four miles distant, in a north-northwesterly direction. The ridge between the forks of the King's rises up in a crest, which, three miles southwest of Camp 180, is 12,400 feet above the sea. From the summit of this ridge there is a precipitous descent to the north, into the cañon of the middle fork, which is, perhaps, even deeper than the one just described.

The crest presents a very serrated outline. Two peaks lying just in front of it are especially fine; they are between five and six miles east of Camp 180; both are probably over 14,000 feet high, the northern being a little the higher. This was named Mount King, and the southern one Mount Gardner. Mount King breaks off in grand precipices on the northwest side, like the Half Dome; these are several thousand feet in height, and almost vertical, producing the effect of an immense obelisk. The annexed woodcut (Fig. 19), from a sketch by Mr. Hoffmann, gives an idea of the form of this grand peak; the point of view was at Camp 180, about six miles west of the summit.

The region around the crest of the ridge between the forks of the King's

Fig. 19.

MOUNT KING, LOOKING EAST, FROM CAMP 180.

consists of granite masses, with spurs projecting out from them, and embracing basins of bare rock, each having a small lake at the bottom. The only living things visible in these valleys are the grasses in the small meadows which border the lakes. Everywhere else are to be seen only smooth, bare rocks, or granitic *débris* in steeply-sloping piles at the base of the precipices. The crests of the ridges are thin and shattered, — so thin that, in some cases, they could only be traversed by hitching the body over while sitting astride of them.

At the head of the north fork, along the main crest of the Sierra, is a range of peaks, from 13,500 to 14,000 feet high, which we called "the Palisades." These were unlike the rest of the crest in outline and color, and were doubtless volcanic; they were very grand and fantastic in shape, like the rocks seen on the Silver Mountain trail near Ebbett's Pass. (See Plate III.) All doubts as to the nature of these peaks were removed after observing on the east side of the crest, in Owen's Valley, vast streams of lava which had flowed down the slope of the Sierra, just below the Palisades.

64

Three days were spent by the party in trying to find some place where the ridge between the forks of the King's could be crossed with animals, so that the party could reach the middle fork and thence make their way to Mount Goddard. This was ascertained to be impossible, and it was found necessary to return to the cañon of the south fork. From here it was, after some hesitation, decided to cross the mountains into Owen's Valley, and, after following it up for forty or fifty miles, to turn west and cross the Sierra again, so as thus to reach the head-waters of the San Joaquin, over a trail which was made, in 1863, by a party of soldiers in pursuit of Indians.

A day and a half was required to make the distance of twelve miles which lay between Camp 179, in the south fork cañon, and the summit of the Sierra; although the labor of crossing was much facilitated by the fact that a party of prospecters had crossed here not long before, and had done a good deal towards making a passable trail. Camp 181, midway between the valley and the summit, was found to be 9,627 feet high. To the north of this camp, and nearly east of Mount King, but on the main crest of the Sierra, was a high, naked rock, rising fully 3,000 feet above the trail at its base, and one of the grandest objects seen among these mountains. The sketch (Fig. 20) will serve to convey a faint idea of its majestic form.

The distance from Camp 181 to the summit was found to be about eight miles. The crest, on the pass, is double, the first summit being 11,031 feet high, and the eastern one 12,057 feet. The latter is a very sharp ridge, with both sides inclined at as steep an angle as the loose materials could maintain without sliding; the actual crest is a sharp comb of rock. The peaks on each side are very steep, and were estimated to be 2,500 feet above the pass, or fully 14,500 feet above the sea. At this time (July 27) there was no snow on the line traversed by our party, although large patches were seen much lower down in shaded localities.

From the crest of the Sierra to its base in Owen's Valley is about eight miles in a direct line, and the average descent is just 1,000 feet per mile for that distance. From the foot of the mountains a gradual and uniform slope extends into the valley, forming an inclined plane, strewn with boulders resting upon a sandy soil. This plain is dry and barren, and covered with the usual desert shrubs, Artemisia, Purshia, Linosyris, and others. The

Fig. 20.

PEAK NEAR CAMP 181.

highest peaks of the main crest are not more than ten or eleven miles from the valley, and fully 10,500 feet above it.

The mountains were entered again at the head of the west branch of Owen's River, on which Camp 187 was situated, at an elevation of 9,298 feet above the sea. To the north of this is an extremely barren table of lava, and on the south granite. The valley of the stream is half a mile wide, and flanked on both sides by beautifully regular moraines, from 1,000 to 1,200 feet above the bottom.

The summit of the Sierra was crossed at an altitude of 12,400 feet, and although the crest rose up in front, appearing as one continuous wall, and seemingly not to be scaled, yet the ascent was found to be on a comparatively easy grade, with the exception of one rocky place near the summit. There is an obscure Indian foot-trail which crosses here, and a body of seventy cavalry, with their pack-train, crossed by it in June, 1863. At that time there were patches of snow half a mile long upon the road. A wagon-road could be made over this pass, without much difficulty; but its great height, and the immense body of snow which must lie here during nearly or quite all the year, forbid the idea of any such undertaking. The crest here is very rugged, rising in precipitous ridges about 1,000 feet above the pass in its immediate vicinity, and perhaps 2,000 feet at a little distance north and south.

The views from the high points above the trail at the summit were of the grandest description. Eight miles to the north was a group of dark, crimson-colored peaks, and twenty-five miles farther in that direction were the snow-clad ranges near Mono Lake. In a southerly direction rose a vast mass of granite peaks and ridges, with the same sharp scattered crests, vertical cliffs overhanging snow-fields and amphitheatres with frozen lakes, which were the main features of the views in the region about the head of King's River.

On the west side of the pass there was one mile of rocky and steep descent; but otherwise no difficulty was experienced. Great slopes were traversed, which were worn and polished by glaciers, and, as everywhere else in the Sierra, these exhibitions of ancient glacial phenomena were exhibited on a much grander scale on the west slope of the Sierra than they had been observed to be on the eastern side.

Camp 188, a little below the summit, was at an elevation of 9,940 feet, and from this high peaks on both sides were ascended and examined. Mr. Gardner visited the crimson-colored group noticed above, and which was about five miles north of the camp. The rocks were found to be of meta-morphic slate, which continues about eight miles to the north, and is there lost under the granite. Enclosed in the slate, and having the same dip and strike, is a vein of white quartz rock sixty to seventy feet wide. The " Red Slate Peaks," as they were called, were found to be about 13,400 feet in elevation. This group forms the northern termination of the great elevated range of the Sierra, which stretches to the south, for a distance of over ninety miles, without any depression below 12,000 feet, in all proba-bility the highest continuous mass of mountains in North America. To the north, between the Red Slate Peaks and the Mono Group, a considerable depression exists, over which is a pass, of the height of which we have no positive knowledge.

There is a great depression where the three largest branches of the King's

On top of Tioga Pass heading west toward Tuolumne Meadows

GEOLOGICAL GROUP

William M. Gabb   J.D. Whitney   Clarence King

Chester Averill   William Ashburner   C.F. Hoffmann   William H. Brewer

come together. In this Camp 189 was made, at a distance of twenty-two miles from the summit of the Sierra, and 6,930 feet above the sea. Grassy meadows occur here, and rising above them are many rocky knolls rounded by former glaciers. This locality has long been a favorite resort of the Indians, on account of its remoteness from the settled part of California, and its consequent security. The abundance of game and the great number of pine trees in this valley also added to its charms. Thousands of trees were seen which had trenches dug around them, to catch the worms which live in the bark, as is said; these, as well as the nuts of the pine, are staple articles of food among the " Diggers." All the movements of our party were watched by the Indians from a distance and signalled by smokes, but no attack was made, as there might have been, had they not been provided with an escort.

From Camp 189 the country to the south was explored, in the direction of Mount Goddard, an important topographical station for connecting with the work on the other side of the King's. In going from Camp 189 to 190 the middle and south forks of the San Joaquin were crossed, and a due south course was kept towards a high point on the ridge, eight miles distant. The valley widens out here, and includes a broad belt of rolling country, with numerous low hills of granite, whose tops and sides are all smoothly rounded by glacial action. The predominant trees here are *Pinus Jeffreyi* and *P. contorta*. As we rise out of the valley, immense moraines are seen at the height of from 1,500 to 2,000 feet above the valley. A glacier, at least 1,500 feet deep, eight or nine miles wide, and probably thirty miles long, perhaps much more, once flowed down this valley, and has left its traces everywhere along its sides.

A peak a little south of Camp 190, and 10,711 feet above the sea, was climbed; from this a grand view of the Sierra between the Obelisk Range and the Mount Brewer Group was obtained. The snow lay on this ridge several hundred feet below the summit; but the *Pinus albicaulis* grows to the very top. This forms one of a series of high points which extend in a line nearly parallel with the crest of the Sierra, and from sixteen to twenty miles distant from it, thus preserving all through this region the same double-crested character which the range has farther south around the head of King's River.

The next move took the party about twelve miles in a southeasterly direction, and to a point only eighteen miles from Mount Goddard. This camp (No. 191) was at an elevation of 10,268 feet. The route followed lay along and over a ridge, with a very sharp crest breaking off in grand precipices on each side. It has also a parapet along the south edge similar to that described as forming the rim of the Kettle; this is in places thirty feet high, and rises like a grand wall, with a narrow shelf on the north; from this there is a very steep slope down for a thousand feet or more.

From Camp 191 an unsuccessful attempt was made to reach Mount Goddard, without the animals, as they could be taken no farther. The only possible way led along the divide between King's and San Joaquin Rivers, over a series of ridges, high and sharp, with valleys between, a thousand feet deep or more, so that progress was excessively slow and tiresome. Cotter and one of the soldiers succeeded, after a day's climbing, in getting within 300 feet of the summit, and hung up the barometer just before it was too dark to see to read it. They were then at an elevation of 13,648 feet, making the height of the mountain about 14,000 feet. The return to an impromptu camp, at an elevation of about 12,000 feet and without provisions or fire, made by the remainder of the party at the base of the mountain, required the whole night, and was hazardous in the extreme.

From Camp 191 the party returned to 189, and from there worked to the northwest in the cañon of the north fork of the San Joaquin. For three fourths of the way the route followed led down the depression at the junction of the three forks before noticed. This depression has the appearance of a valley only when seen from the heights around it. There are numerous flats lying between rounded hills of bare granite; these flats are sometimes covered by forests, but many of them form beautiful open meadows in which many thousand cattle might be pastured.

The north fork of the San Joaquin comes down through a very deep cañon, and the wide, open, valley-like depression terminates here. This cañon is from 3,000 to 4,000 feet deep, and proved to be a serious obstacle to the advance of the party. Near the junction of the north and main forks it is a mere notch, and its walls exhibit some grandly picturesque features. Two or three miles southeast of this is a most remarkable dome, more perfect in its form than any before seen in the State. It rises to the height of 1,800 feet above the river, and presents exactly the appearance of the upper part of a sphere; or, as Professor Brewer says, "of the top of a gigantic balloon struggling to get up through the rock."

Camp 194, in the cañon, was at an altitude of about 4,750 feet, while the ranges to the east and northeast rose from 4,000 to 5,000 feet above this, and those on the west about 3,000 feet. The sides of the cañon are very abrupt, and present immense surfaces of naked granite, resembling the valley of the Yosemite. There are everywhere in this valley the traces of former glaciers, on an immense scale, and as the party rose above the cañon on the north, in leaving the river, the moraine on the opposite side was seen very distinctly, and appeared to be at an elevation of not less than 3,000 feet above the bottom of the valley. It was evident that the glaciers which came down the various branches of the San Joaquin all united here to form one immense "sea of ice," which filled the whole of the wide depression spoken of above, and left its moraines at this high elevation above the present river-bed.

The party passed out of the cañon to the northwest, first ascending a steep ridge, over 3,000 feet high, and then entering a wide elevated valley, where Camp 195 was made, at an elevation of about 7,250 feet. On the high ridge traversed in getting to this camp were many boulders of lava, which must have been brought from some more northerly point and dropped in their present position by ancient glaciers. The source of these boulders seems to have been near Mount Clark, in the Obelisk Range. The view from the summit of the ridge was a grand one, commanding the whole of the Mount Lyell and Obelisk Groups, as well as the main range of the Sierra to the east, where are many dark-colored peaks, apparently volcanic. A very high and massive peak was seen to the east of Mount Lyell, which has since been named by us Mount Ritter, and is believed to be the dominating point of the group (see page 109).

In the depression to the west of the ridge noticed above are heavy forests and fine meadows scattered over the country, into which many cattle had been driven from Fresno County, to escape the extreme drought of the season. The meadows occupy the flats or level intervals between the domes of granite; grassy "flats," as they are called, occur everywhere along the Sierra at about this altitude, on the high lands between the large streams.

Camp 196, a few miles north of 195, was at the base of a prominent peak, which was supposed to belong to the Obelisk Group, for which the party was aiming. On ascending it, however, it was found to be about ten miles due south of the Obelisk. It was found to be 10,950 feet high and commanded a fine view. This is called Black Mountain on the map accompanying the present volume. Eighteen miles northeast of this is the lowest gap or pass over the Sierra which occurs between Carson's and Walker's Passes, a distance of about 250 miles. An approximation to its height was obtained by an observation of the barometer on the peak ascended near Camp 195, at a point which was ascertained by levelling to be at about the same altitude as the pass itself. The result of the calculation gave 9,200 feet as the height of the summit of the pass, which is considerably lower than the Mono Pass. Cattle have been driven across to Owen's Valley over this route, the north fork of the San Joaquin being crossed at a point much farther up than where our party traversed it, and where the cañon is not nearly so deep.

From Camp 196 the party made their way, as rapidly as the worn-out condition of the men and horses permitted, to Clark's ranch, on the trail from Mariposa to the Yosemite. They first travelled in a southwesterly direction, over a region of dome-shaped granite hills, for a distance of twenty-three miles, and camped at the head of the Chiquito San Joaquin, and at the altitude of 7,463 feet. Many meadows were passed, into which large numbers of cattle had been driven. One of these is known as Neal's ranch, or Jackass Meadows. From this point there were trails which could be followed, and this was the first sign of a return to the regions of civilization.